BREAKOUT BIOGRAPHIES

MICHAEL PHELPS

Greatest

Swimmer

of All Time

Ryan Nagelhout

PowerKiDS
press.

New York

Published in 2018 by The Rosen Publishing Group, Inc.
29 East 21st Street, New York, NY 10010

First Edition

Editor: Elizabeth Krajnik
Book Design: Tanya Dellaccio

Photo Credits: Cover Donald Miralle/Sports Illustrated/Getty Images; cover, back cover, pp. 1, 3, 4, 6, 8, 10, 12, 14, 16, 18, 20, 22, 24, 26, 28, 30–32 ninanaina/Shutterstock.com; p. 5 Chris Hyde/Getty Images Sport/Getty Images; p. 7 (top) JEWEL SAMAD/AFP/Getty Images; p. 7 (bottom) Frazer Harrison/Getty Images Entertainment/Getty Images; p. 9 Nick Laham/ Getty Images Sport/Getty Images; p. 11 (top) Ross Kinnaird/Allsport/Getty Images Sport/Getty Images; p. 11 (bottom) https://commons.wikimedia.org/wiki/File:Fireworks,_Sydney_Harbour_Bridge,_ 2000_Summer_Olympics_closing_ceremony.jpg; p. 13 (top) Adam Pretty/Getty Images Sport/ Getty Images; p. 13 (bottom) Shaun Botterill/Getty Images Sport/Getty Images; pp. 15 (top), 17 (bottom) Al Bello/Getty Images Sport/Getty Images; p. 15 (bottom) TIM CLARY/AFP/Getty Images; p. 17 (top) Richard Heathcote/Getty Images Sport/Getty Images; pp. 19 (top), 23 Heinz Kluetmeier/ Sports Illustrated/Getty Images; p. 19 (bottom) Chris Graythen/Getty Images Sport/Getty Images; p. 21 (top) Chris Trotman/Getty Images Sport/Getty Images; p. 21 (bottom) John Biever/Sports Illustrated/ Getty Images; p. 25 (both) MARTIN BUREAU/AFP/Getty Images; p. 27 ODD ANDERSEN/AFP/ Getty Images; p. 29 (top) Bryan Bedder/Getty Images Entertainment/Getty Images; p. 29 (bottom) Jeff Zelevansky/Getty Images Sport/Getty Images.

Cataloging-in-Publication Data

Names: Nagelhout, Ryan.
Title: Michael Phelps / Ryan Nagelhout.
Description: New York : PowerKids Press, 2018. | Series: Breakout biographies | Includes index.
Identifiers: ISBN 9781508160663 (pbk.) | ISBN 9781508160687 (library bound) | ISBN 9781508160670 (6 pack)
Subjects: LCSH: Phelps, Michael, 1985–Juvenile literature. | Swimmers–United States–Biography–Juvenile literature. | Olympics–Juvenile literature.
Classification: LCC GV838.P54 N34 2018 | DDC 797.2'1092–dc23

Manufactured in China

CONTENTS

THE BEST EVER

When Michael Fred Phelps II was born on June 30, 1985, his parents Fred and Debbie Phelps had no idea their youngest child would go on to be the greatest swimmer of all time. But Michael would indeed be special, and he took to swimming at an early age.

Phelps started swimming because his sisters, Hilary and Whitney, joined a local swim team. However, he didn't get serious about the sport until after he watched the 1996 Summer Olympics in Atlanta, Georgia.

Swimming made Phelps world famous. It transformed the tall and skinny kid into an American hero as a teenager and guided his journey into adulthood. Michael Phelps is the greatest swimmer ever, but there's much more to his story than laps and gold medals.

Phelps's parents were dedicated to their children's love of swimming. They moved from one town to another in order to be closer to the kids' swim club.

BALTIMORE BOY

Michael grew up in Baltimore, Maryland. He was an active child, racing around to keep up with his older sisters. He started swimming at age 7 when his sisters joined a swim team. But the sport became more important as he grew older and his behavior started causing problems.

In school, Phelps had trouble focusing on his schoolwork. He couldn't pay attention, and he often bothered kids or talked too much in class. When Phelps was nine years old, he was tested and **diagnosed** with **attention deficit hyperactivity disorder**, or ADHD. Some children battle ADHD's effects by taking part in activities that have structure and **discipline**, such as sports. Phelps played sports, including lacrosse, baseball, and cross-country running. He also took medication and tried to eat a healthy diet, avoiding sugary foods.

Debbie Phelps is active with ADHD Moms, an online community that helps mothers of children diagnosed with ADHD and provides them with resources.

ADHD

ADHD is a disorder that millions of children and adults in the United States live with. Phelps took medication for about four years after he was diagnosed, but at age 13, with his doctor's approval, he thought he could learn to focus and stopped taking his medication. "Your mind is the strongest medicine you can have," he wrote in his autobiography *No Limits*. "You can overcome anything if you think you can and you want to." Phelps credits swimming with helping him control his ADHD without using medication.

DEBBIE PHELPS

STANDING OUT

Phelps's early swimming lessons were tough. At first, he was afraid to put his head underwater, so a teacher told him to lie back and float until he was comfortable. Soon enough, he was learning swimming strokes, including the backstroke and breaststroke. He trained hard and started to swim very well. By age 10, Phelps held the national record in the 100-meter butterfly for boys 10 and under.

In 1996, a senior coach at the North Baltimore Aquatic Club named Bob Bowman spotted Phelps swimming. Bowman noticed Phelps's talent in the water and told his parents he had a gift that could get him into the Olympics. Bowman became Michael's coach, and the two have worked together ever since. Bowman inspired Phelps to train to compete against the best swimmers in the world.

Bowman has been a father figure to Phelps since the two started working together. Phelps's father was not around much when Phelps was growing up.

TEEN OLYMPIAN

Phelps's parents divorced in 1994, and Michael and his sisters lived with their mother in Baltimore. He went to Towson High School and graduated in 2003. By then, he was already an Olympian. At 15 years old, Phelps swam for Team USA at the 2000 Summer Olympics in Sydney, Australia. He was the youngest American male swimmer to compete in the Olympics in 68 years. He finished fifth in the 200-meter butterfly event.

Though Phelps was already one of the best swimmers in the world as a teenager, he was still a normal kid. One of his teachers recalls him running into a classroom door. When the teacher pointed out he was an Olympic athlete, Phelps said, "I'm not that good on land!"

Phelps's performance at the Sydney Olympics made many people very excited about his future swimming career.

2000 SUMMER OLYMPICS CLOSING CEREMONY

STRIKING GOLD

In 2001, Phelps won a gold medal in the 200-meter butterfly event at the Phillips 66 Summer National Championships in Fresno, California. It was the first of many medals he would win as part of Team USA. This swim also broke the world record in the event, making Phelps the youngest person to set a world swimming record. He was 15 years and 9 months old. Phelps then broke his own record and won his first international medal at the 2001 FINA World Aquatics Championships in Fukuoka, Japan.

The Baltimore Bullet continued to shine in competitions for Team USA, helping set a world record in the 4x100-meter medley **relay** at the 2002 Pan Pacific Championships and setting other new records. He also prepared for the next Olympics, which would be held in 2004 in Athens, Greece. It was during these Olympic Games that Phelps's career really took off.

In 2003, Phelps won six medals at the FINA World Aquatics Championships in Barcelona, Spain, and broke world records in the 200-meter butterfly, 200-meter individual medley (IM), and 400-meter IM events.

13

GREEK GOD

Michael Phelps finally struck Olympic gold in 2004. In fact, he struck gold six times! The 19-year-old collected eight medals at the Summer Olympics in Athens, Greece. Phelps won gold and broke his own 400-meter IM world record by 0.15 seconds. He also won gold in the 100-meter butterfly, the 200-meter butterfly, and the 200-meter IM. Phelps and his teammates won gold in the 4x200-meter freestyle relay and the 4x100-meter medley relay.

Phelps also won bronze medals in the 200-meter freestyle and the 4x100-meter freestyle relay. Although Phelps wasn't able to achieve his goal of breaking American swimmer Mark Spitz's record of seven gold medals in a single Olympiad, he was officially a world-famous superstar. International Olympic Committee president Jacques Rogge called Phelps "the icon of the games."

In pursuit of his goal of eight gold medals in a single Olympiad, Phelps set one world record and three Olympic records in the pool at the Athens Olympics.

"The Thorpedo"

Phelps admired Australian swimmer Ian Thorpe, who was called "the Thorpedo" because of his speed in the pool. It was Thorpe to whom Phelps lost in the 200-meter freestyle in 2004. Phelps finished behind Thorpe and Pieter van den Hoogenband in the event many called "The Race of the Century." Phelps didn't let his loss get to him, though. He later used Thorpe as **motivation** to crush a number of records, including Thorpe's world record in the 200-meter freestyle, at the 2007 FINA World Aquatics Championships in Melbourne, Australia.

IAN THORPE

WHY SO FAST?

By age 19, Phelps was one of the best swimmers in the world. But what makes him so fast in the water? Phelps is 6 feet 4 inches (193 cm) tall. His **wingspan** is 6 feet 8 inches long (203.2 cm). That's 4 inches (10.2 cm) longer than his body! Many human beings have about the same wingspan and height, and some scientists think this difference allows Phelps to reach farther and push himself through water faster.

Phelps's large feet act like flippers in the pool, and he's also double-jointed, which means his ankles can bend farther than most swimmers' ankles. Some think this flexibility is a big factor in his ability to go farther with each stroke.

Whether it's body type or hard work that makes Phelps great, both scientists and swimming fans marvel at his abilities in the pool.

SCIENCE AT WORK

Some scientists disagree about whether being double-jointed or having a long wingspan makes a true difference in the pool. One scientist interviewed by *Scientific American* in 2008 suggested that Phelps's "stroke mechanics," or the science behind how Phelps moves his arms while swimming, contribute to his amazing success. He also claimed that some swimmers have better "locomotive genius," or a sense of how water moves around them and how it impacts their swimming. He hinted that years of training—not just body type—make the true difference for athletes.

Phelps's success in Athens made him a household name around the world. He appeared on television in the United States and continued to get **endorsement** deals with big-name companies. He won five gold medals and one silver medal at the 2005 FINA World Aquatics Championships in Montreal, Canada. He repeated that accomplishment at the 2006 Pan Pacific Swimming Championships in Victoria, British Columbia, Canada. At this competition, he set world records in the 200-meter butterfly, 200-meter IM, and 4x100-meter freestyle.

At the 2007 FINA World Aquatics Championships in Melbourne, Australia, Phelps won seven gold medals. All of these competitions were in preparation for the 2008 Summer Olympics in Beijing, China. Phelps hoped to win eight gold medals there and break Spitz's record. However,

Ian Thorpe doubted that he or anyone else could win eight gold medals at one Olympics. This doubt drove Phelps to train harder than ever before to achieve his goal of breaking Spitz's record.

FINDING TROUBLE

Just weeks after his eight-medal victory in Greece, Phelps was driving when he didn't stop at a stop sign and was pulled over by the police. He had been drinking at a party in Salisbury, Maryland. He was arrested and charged with driving while intoxicated. Phelps was sentenced to 18 months **probation** and fined $250. Phelps later spoke at schools to educate students about how dangerous alcohol and driving while drunk can be. He described it as an "**isolated** incident" and apologized for letting his family, and himself, down.

THE GREAT HAUL

August 17, 2008, was a fateful day for Phelps. His dream of breaking Spitz's record of winning seven gold medals in a single Olympiad became a reality. During the Beijing games, Michael Phelps had the greatest individual Olympic Games in history. He won eight gold medals in a week, including those for the 200-meter butterfly and the 4x200-meter freestyle relay on the same day. In addition to winning all those medals, Phelps set seven world records and one Olympic record.

Phelps's eight medals are known as the "Great Haul of China," a reference to the country's Great Wall. Fittingly, Ian Thorpe was in Beijing to see Phelps win his eighth gold and shook Phelps's hand after the race. "I am so happy to have been proved wrong," Thorpe said.

For breaking Mark Spitz's world record and winning eight gold medals in Beijing, Phelps got a $1 million bonus from Speedo, one of his sponsors.

PUTTING HIS MONEY TO GOOD USE

Phelps used his $1 million bonus to start the Michael Phelps Foundation, which donates money to programs that educate people about water safety and help kids get involved with swimming. One of his first actions with the foundation was a tour to eight cities across the United States, during which Phelps educated young swimmers about how to lead healthy, happy lives outside the pool. Phelps said that the foundation was a way for him to give back to the sport that had shaped his life.

In 2009, trouble managed to find Phelps once again. A British newspaper published photos of Phelps smoking a recreational drug called marijuana. Phelps was embarrassed by the **scandal** and apologized. USA Swimming suspended Phelps from competing for three months and Kellogg, one of his sponsors, didn't renew his contract.

Ryan Lochte, a new American swimming star, was seemingly surpassing Phelps's talent. Lochte beat Phelps in the 200-meter freestyle and the 200-meter IM at the 2011 FINA World Championships in Shanghai, China. Despite losing to Lochte in two events, Phelps took home gold medals in the 100-meter butterfly, the 200-meter butterfly, the 4x200-meter freestyle relay, and the 4x100-meter medley relay. He also won bronze in the 4x100-meter freestyle relay. With the next Olympiad just a year away, Phelps needed to focus to

Although Lochte was now a serious rival of Phelps's in the pool, the two swimmers are friends. At swim meets they often play cards together and listen to the same music.

CALLING
IT QUITS

Phelps swam in his fourth Olympics in London, England, in 2012. There, he made more history, becoming an 18-time gold medalist. Phelps won four gold medals and two silver medals in London, giving him 22 Olympic medals overall, a new record. The former record holder was gymnast Larisa Latynina with 18 total medals.

After the London Olympics, Phelps announced that he would retire from swimming because he found it harder to recover as he got older. But his retirement only lasted two years. In April 2014, Phelps announced that he would come out of retirement and return to competitive swimming. At his first major event, the 2014 Pan Pacific Swimming Championships in Gold Coast, Queensland, Australia, Phelps won three gold medals and two silver medals to

After winning gold in the men's 4x100-meter medley relay at the London Olympics, Phelps received a trophy from the Fédération Internationale de Natation, or FINA, for being the most decorated Olympic athlete. The trophy says, "To Michael Phelps, the greatest Olympic athlete of all time."

LAST LAPS

After announcing that he would come out of retirement in April, Phelps hit rock bottom. He was arrested for driving drunk on September 30, 2014. USA Swimming suspended him for six months and he wasn't allowed to compete on the 2015 World Championship team. Phelps called it the lowest point in his life.

Despite the setback, Phelps came back and trained harder than ever. He qualified for his fifth Olympics at the U.S. Olympic swimming trials in Omaha, Nebraska, in 2016. Phelps was on the road to Rio de Janeiro, Brazil, and the 2016 Summer Olympics.

In Rio, Phelps won five gold medals and one silver medal. Phelps officially retired with 28 Olympic medals—23 of them gold. He retired for good as the most decorated Olympic athlete of all time.

After the Rio games finished, Phelps joined his coach, Bob Bowman, as a volunteer assistant coach at Arizona State University. He also said he plans to spend time with his wife, Nicole, and their son, Boomer.

A LASTING LEGACY

Because Phelps's career took off when he was so young, he's using his retirement to volunteer, travel, play golf, and run his baby's Instagram. Even out of the pool, Phelps continues to inspire the next generation of American athletes. The Michael Phelps Foundation "Dream Plan Reach" program strives to get kids comfortable in the water, teach them how to swim, and provide them with a pastime they can enjoy. It encourages them to reach for the stars.

"Swimming's been a part of my life for so long. I'm out of the pool, competitively, but I'm still helping," Phelps said in 2016. "The only reason I got in the water was my mom wanted me to just learn how to swim." Phelps hopes his story will not only inspire others but help save lives.

Though he has officially retired from competitive swimming, Phelps stays busy with his foundation and his family.

FAMILY FIRST

Despite retiring at age 31, Phelps has managed to stay busy. His son, Boomer, was born in May 2016. Phelps said his success in the pool doesn't compare to fatherhood. He called it the "best feeling I have ever felt in my life." In November, three months after his final Olympics, a news source revealed that Phelps and his **fiancée**, Nicole, were already married. The two had a small private wedding ceremony on June 13, 2016, just months before the Rio games began.

MICHAEL, NICOLE, AND BOOMER

TIMELINE

June 30, 1985 — Michael Fred Phelps II is born in Baltimore, Maryland.

1999 — Phelps makes the U.S. National B Team.

2000 — Phelps makes his Olympic debut in Sydney, Australia. He finishes fifth in the 200-meter butterfly event.

2001 — Phelps sets the world record for the 200-meter butterfly event. He later breaks his own record at the 2001 World Championships.

2003 — Phelps graduates from Towson High School.

2004 — Phelps wins six gold medals and two bronze medals at the Summer Olympics in Athens, Greece.

2004 — Phelps begins taking classes and training at University of Michigan in Ann Arbor.

2008 — Phelps breaks Mark Spitz's world record by winning eight gold medals at the Summer Olympics in Beijing, China.

2008 — Phelps is named *Sports Illustrated*'s Sportsman of the Year and launches the Michael Phelps Foundation.

2012 — Phelps wins four gold medals and two silver medals at the Summer Olympics in London, England.

2012 — Phelps announces his retirement from competitive swimming.

2014 — Phelps ends his retirement and swims at U.S. National competitions.

August 2016 — Phelps wins five gold medals and one silver medal at the Summer Olympics in Rio de Janeiro, Brazil.

2016 — Phelps officially retires from competitive swimming.

GLOSSARY

attention deficit hyperactivity disorder (ADHD): A common disorder with which people have trouble paying attention, can't calm down, or are impulsive.

diagnose: To recognize a disease by signs and symptoms.

discipline: Control that is gained through insisting that rules be followed.

endorsement: A kind of public approval or support.

fiancée: A woman engaged to be married.

isolated: Being alone or apart.

motivation: The act or process of giving someone a reason for doing something.

probation: A period of time in which a person who has broken the law is watched and must behave well in order not to be punished more seriously.

relay: A race between teams in which each team member swims a different part of the race.

scandal: An occurrence in which people are shocked and upset because of behavior that is morally or legally wrong.

wingspan: The distance from the tip of one hand to the tip of the other hand when the arms are stretched out to the side

INDEX

WEBSITES

Due to the changing nature of Internet links, PowerKids Press has
developed an online list of websites related to the subject of this book.
This site is updated regularly. Please use this link to access the list:
www.powerkidslinks.com/bbios/phelps